Original title:
The Beauty of the Sea Urchin

Copyright © 2025 Creative Arts Management OÜ
All rights reserved.

Author: Adeline Fairfax
ISBN HARDBACK: 978-1-80587-280-1
ISBN PAPERBACK: 978-1-80587-750-9

Iridescent Armor

In ocean's depths, they wear their shades,
Like tiny knights in prickly parades.
With spikes so sharp, they claim their turf,
Dancing 'round like they're on a surf.

Shimmering Shadows

They twirl and spin in underwater dance,
Grinning with shells, they take their chance.
A pop of color, a laugh, a cheer,
Those little guys don't shed a tear!

A Spiny Serenade

Singing songs in their pokey attire,
With every bob, they spark our desire.
Who knew such spines could bring us glee,
In this comedy of sea and spree?

The Enchantment of Spines

Oh, the wonders of these prickly charms,
They entertain us with their little farms.
With a giggle here and a poke there,
These regal critters, we gladly stare!

Twilight Shadows on Sandy Beds

In the twilight, shapes appear,
Spiky dancers without fear.
They roll and tumble through the sand,
With little legs that wave and stand.

Underneath the moon's soft glow,
They flaunt their colors, put on a show.
A little prickly ball of fun,
Fashioning jokes just for a pun.

Pastel Portraits of the Deep

Oh, vibrant colors never cease,
Like candy sprinkles in the breeze.
They hide in rocks, a mismatched crew,
Making odd faces, just for you.

Pastels bright, like a candy shop,
While their prickles give a little bop.
Who painted these, it's hard to tell,
A wacky artist with a shell.

Dancers in the Marine Ballet

In ocean currents, they start to swirl,
Little pirouettes, what a whirl!
With each embrace of the sea's cool air,
They strike a pose with utmost flair.

A rippling dance in coral trails,
Mimicking fish with silly tails.
If laughter could bubble up and sing,
These spiky friends would wear the ring.

Nature's Artistry in Hidden Depths

Deep in the water, art does hide,
With prickly shells, all magnified.
Collecting giggles like seaweed strands,
From sandy beds to far-off lands.

A masterpiece of funny quirks,
They charm the crabs, make friends with perks.
In nature's theater, they steal the scene,
Whimsical wonders, all in between.

The Hidden Ballet

In a dance of spines they twirl,
A waltz under the ocean swirl.
With pirouettes on coral's edge,
They leap and bounce without a hedge.

A quirky crew in shells adorned,
With little moves, they'd be well-horned.
With seaweed fans, they take the stage,
Each performance, a humorous page.

Reflections of a Briny Heart

In tides that tease and tickle toes,
A heart that beats where the ocean flows.
Waves whisper secrets, oh so sly,
As sea urchins grin at the passersby.

Caught in a wave, they laugh so loud,
In watery frolics, they feel so proud.
Their prickly coats, a fashion choice,
In the briny deep, they sing with voice.

Tactile Treasures Beneath Waves

Beneath the surf, with curious grace,
Nestle odd shapes in a warm embrace.
With tiny spikes, they poke and prod,
Creating fun, that feels so odd.

Like spiky balls from Neptune's game,
They bounce around without much shame.
In every crack where they reside,
A comical world where giggles hide.

Chronicles of the Sea's Palette

In hues of purple, green, and blue,
Urchins proudly flaunt their crew.
Painting the sea with a splash of cheer,
A whimsical sight that's so sincere.

With a grin made of shells not quite round,
They concoct antics without a sound.
In this underwater artful spree,
Every prickly ball lives merrily free.

Oceanic Treasures Revealed

Beneath the waves, quite round and spiny,
They wiggle and jiggle, looking all whiny.
A curious critter, fashionably dressed,
In armor and colors, they're simply the best.

They don't have a brain, but they sure do pose,
With prickly apparel, they strike quite a pose.
On ocean's stage, they steal the scene,
In their little homes, they're always serene.

Encased in Ocean's Mystery

Hiding in shells, like a child at play,
Pretending to be rocks, day after day.
When you spot them glimmer, just take a look,
With quirky charm, they're off the hook!

They roll and they tumble, with grace they prance,
In a dance made of water, they take a chance.
Laughing with bubbles, they're masters of fun,
In the ocean's playground, they're number one!

Silent Guardians of the Shoreline

On sandy shores, they claim their space,
With a prickly grin upon their face.
Guardians of secrets, silent and sly,
Just don't poke them—oh my, oh my!

They sit there waiting, with patience untold,
Wishing for sand castles made of gold.
With each rolling wave, they giggle and sigh,
Waving goodbye to a seagull nearby.

Elegance in Echinoderm Form

In fashion so unique, they strut in style,
Each stunning spire making us smile.
With a flair for the colorful, oh so bright,
Even crabs pause to admire their sight.

They shimmy and shake in the currents' flow,
With a wink and a nod, they steal the show.
From rocky facades to coral frays,
These spiny delights brighten our days.

Texture of Life Beneath the Waves

In the depths where spines do play,
A fuzzy ball rolls, bright and gay.
Tickling fish go on their way,
Avoiding hugs that might betray.

Beneath the sea's whimsical whim,
They sport their crowns, quite on a whim.
Wiggly fools in a watery gym,
Chasing laughter on a fin.

Wonders in a Sea of Thorns

With pointy bits and prickly charm,
They seem to wink, 'We're here, no harm!'
Dancing close, a little alarm,
A poke from them? It's quite the balm!

In currents strong they twist and twirl,
A spiral dance—a spiky whirl.
Jellyfish giggle, oh what a pearl,
In this ocean of quirk, they unfurl.

Luminescent Spines and Shadows

Glowing in the dark, oh what a sight,
A prickly creature with sheer delight.
They giggle softly, arms out tight,
Generating laughs in the moonlight.

When shadows loom and tides do sway,
They flash those spines in a cheeky way.
Beneath the waves, they laugh and play,
A comedy show at the close of day.

Sunlight on a Spiny Back

In the sun, a spiky ball waits,
Prickly but cute, it just captivates.
Wobbling around like a tiny clown,
A throne of thorns in an underwater gown.

With a grin that says, 'Come tickle me!',
Not the best decision, wait and see.
It spins and rolls in a silly dance,
Creating laughter with every chance.

A Touch of the Abyss

Down below, where darkness creeps,
Lurks a creature that rarely sleeps.
It peeks out from its prickly fort,
A spined surprise on seafloor's court.

With a curious vibe, it looks about,
In ocean's quiet, it gives a shout.
'Got any snacks for a hungry mate?'
While dodging fish on a dinner plate!

Colors of the Hidden Depths

Bright hues splash from where it lies,
A rainbow of points beneath the skies.
Each color strange, a quirky trend,
A walking art that won't pretend.

With polka dots and stripes so bold,
Who knew the deep could be this gold?
Gather 'round for a colorful show,
Nature's punchline puts on a glow!

Guardian of the Ocean Bed

A knight with spikes on a sandy quest,
Defending seas with a wobbly jest.
It guards its turf with a playful air,
Yet tickle its spine and it won't care!

With a flip and a twist, it takes a stand,
In this wacky world, it's the king of the sand.
Whoever thought a creature so small,
Could be the jester of this watery hall!

Secrets of the Tide Pools

In tiny homes where critters play,
Spiky balls have much to say.
They wiggle and squirm, it's quite a sight,
With pincers and colors, oh what a fright!

They hide beneath with glee and pride,
In pools of wonders, they like to hide.
Tickle their spines, just don't get poked,
These prickly friends delight with jokes they've choked!

A Dance Among the Rocks

Bouncing around like a wobbly ball,
These quirky beings have no fear at all.
With an awkward sway and a careful flip,
They pirouette past with a tiny yip!

Green and purple, dressed in style,
They whirl and twirl, oh what a mile!
Caught in a current, they roll and spin,
Life in the tide pools, let the fun begin!

Intricacies in the Sand

Buried treasure, just a glance,
Watch them peek out, give you a chance.
With little legs and a whole lotta flair,
They dance in the surf without a care!

Each tiny bump tells a tale untold,
Of underwater stories that can unfold.
With a laugh and a wiggle, they start to show,
The joys of the ocean, come join the show!

Spiked Wonders of the Deep

Under the waves, they proudly sit,
With spindly arms, they're quite the wit.
A crown of spikes, they wear with glee,
"Don't touch me, friend, I'm prickly as can be!"

They chuckle softly in the salty breeze,
With every wave, they float with ease.
The artists of ocean, each color bright,
A spiky delight, oh what a sight!

Nature's Spiny Treasure

In the tide pools they do hide,
With spines that poke and prickle wide.
They sport a look, both odd and grand,
Nature's joke, a spiny band.

Little round balls, so sly and spry,
Rolling on the ocean floor, oh my!
A treasure chest of quirks galore,
Who knew the sea held this much more?

Silent Guardians of the Shore

Watch them stand in silent pride,
Guardians of the ocean tide.
With a fortress made of spikes, it seems,
They're living out our wildest dreams.

Poking fun at beachgoer's toes,
In camouflage, they strike a pose.
A hidden gem, a prickly friend,
Vigilant until the very end.

Ocean's Porcupine

In a shell that's round, they dwell with glee,
A fuzzy spiked ball, oh what a spree!
Nature's porcupine, they stand quite proud,
Making waves, attracting a crowd.

With vibrant colors, they catch the eye,
While pretending to be shy, oh my!
They tickle the toes of unsuspecting peas,
In their quirkiness, they aim to please.

Mysterious Spines and Vibrant Hues

With colors that dazzle, they float about,
Mysterious spines, there's little doubt.
A dance of hues in the salty brine,
Who knew these critters could look so fine?

Look closely and you might just see,
A grin beneath their spiky spree.
They wiggle and giggle in their own way,
Making the underwater world a play!

Guardians of the Reef

In the ocean depths, they roam,
With tiny spikes—away from home.
They wear their armor, looking keen,
Watch out, they're not just a green bean!

Bouncing along with a curious flair,
They wiggle and giggle with salty care.
With eyes like buttons, they wave with pride,
Guardians of the reef, they cannot hide.

Enigmatic Creatures Below

Crawling slowly, beneath the tide,
With fashion sense, they take great pride.
No heels or caps, just prickles galore,
Dancing their dance, what's behind their door?

Charismatic yet spiky, oh what a mix,
They charm the fish with some tricky tricks.
In the kingdom of coral, they reign supreme,
Living out loud in a spiky dream.

Nature's Prickly Poetry

On the ocean floor, they tell their tale,
Spiky sonnets on a sandy trail.
With each little poke and a tiny smile,
They make the sea laugh, oh what a style!

Crafting their verses with bubbles and foam,
Prickly poets, they call the ocean home.
Inky-black ink maybe, or shells so fine,
Each little creature has a story to shine.

Tidal Dreams

In the midst of the splash and the spray,
They dream of adventures, come what may.
With twirls and swirls beneath the wave,
A life in the sea is nothing but brave!

Dreamy little ones, in the brine they dart,
With currents and tides, they make their art.
Each wave a canvas, each splash a cheer,
Oh little enigmas, we hold you dear.

Spiny Schemes

Whispers of mischief on the ocean floor,
Planning their dance for a seaweedy tour.
They laugh at the fish with their spiky wit,
Crafting their schemes in a bubble-bit!

With wiggly toes and spiky hairstyles,
They prance through the tides, here come the smiles!
Sailing the currents, they giggle and squeal,
In their underwater realm, they seal the deal.

Inspirations from the Ocean Floor

In a world where spines decide,
A urchin's giggles cannot hide.
With prickly hats and a bouncy poise,
They bask in seaweed, laughing with joys.

They roll on rocks like tiny kings,
Wielding crowns made of spiky things.
Oh what a sight, a fuzzy crew,
Dancing under waves of blue.

Now some may think they're pretty brash,
But what do you know? They're just a splash!
With shells that twirk and swirl and spin,
In a fun, flamboyant ocean grin.

So here's to those who roam the sand,
With spiky fun they take a stand.
In ocean depths, with smiles so wide,
They're the quirky pride of ocean's tide.

Nature's Hidden Delights

In the underwater world so bright,
Are creatures that give quite a fright!
Spines and colors, they dance and twirl,
In their own unique, muddy whirl.

With little eyes that peek out shy,
They tell the ocean, 'Watch me fly!'
Blowing bubbles and making jokes,
These spiky pals are no mere folks.

In tides that tickle and current that tease,
They do their best to charm with ease.
Sprinkled secrets in each wave's flow,
For laughter echoes from down below!

So when you wander where waters be,
Keep an eye out for glee's decree.
For hidden treasures that sparkle and beam,
Are nature's gems, living the dream!

Kaleidoscope of the Deep

In the depths where colors collide,
Lives a creature with a spiky pride.
Each angle boasts a fun new face,
Designs that put mere shells to disgrace.

With hues that dance as they find their spots,
Turning tides to vibrant dots.
One moment they're purple; the next, they're green,
A spiky party, oh what a scene!

Pinch your arm, oh, are they rough!
Yet their antics say, 'We're cool and tough!'
Beneath the waves, they jiggle and sway,
Bringing smiles in their own odd way.

So dive below, don't be shy,
Where these pointy pals laugh and fly.
In the kaleidoscope, what a delight,
Join the fun; it feels just right!

A Sonnet of Spines

Tiny creatures on the ocean bed,
With spines that tickle like jokes from a friend.
Bouncing about, they dance with glee,
In a shimmery world, they are fancy and free.

Who knew elegance could come with a poke?
With laughter and waves, they play and they joke.
In shells so bright, they wear their best,
An underwater comedy, they love to jest.

With every tumble, giggles abound,
As they whirl through the water, with merriment found.
Their prickly exteriors hold treasures untold,
In the heart of the ocean, bold stories unfold.

So here's to the spines, oh what a sight!
Life's funniest jesters, beneath waves of delight.

Vestiges of Ancient Seas

In spiky coats of purple hue,
They waddle 'round like little shrews!
With shells that look like tiny hats,
Pretending they're the ocean's chats.

Tall tales told in ocean's brine,
In riddles danced, they sip their wine.
Prancing 'round on sandy floors,
Nature's jesters, never boars!

A culinary delicacy, too—
Eaten raw, for brave of hue!
Yet you'd think they'd stay and fight,
But they just roll away from sight.

Some think they're magnets for our feet,
But these little guys can't take the heat.
Dancing while the currents sway,
Poking fun on ocean's play!

Timeless Wonders in the Surge

Uplifted by the playful swell,
They twist and turn, a living spell.
Each spiny tip, a secret grin,
Who knew the ocean held such kin?

Like round little aliens on parade,
With colors that would never fade.
They know how to steal the show,
While silently moving to and fro.

Sprinkled 'round the rocky shore,
They play coy behind a rocky door.
Oh, what mischief they proclaim,
As if they're all in this grand game!

With a wink and a playful wink,
They often give us space to think.
Should we dance or should we play?
Let's just clash in a silly way!

Nature's Armor: A Canvas of Color

With coats of crayons, colors bright,
They flaunt their styles, day and night.
Each prickly patch a work of art,
Looks like they took a trip to a mart.

Floating 'round like floaty phones,
With all their groans and squeaky tones.
They giggle as the waves do crash,
In their colorful armored stash.

If sea cucumbers were to boast,
These little gems would win the toast!
Clashing colors, here they stand,
Beacons of joy on the sand!

Artistically alive and spry,
Creating magic with a sly cry.
In each little form, a chuckle gleams,
Like children lost in painted dreams!

Whims of the Sea's Design

Whimsical shapes against the tide,
They bounce and sway with ocean's guide.
Who knew the sea had such a flair?
With quirky quirks and spiky hair!

They tumble 'long the ocean's way,
Like kooky clowns at a cabaret.
Those tiny critters roll with glee,
In a raucous dance, oh can't you see?

With peeks of colors, oh so bright,
They make a jester's choice in sight.
You'd think they're lost, yet never roam,
Just having fun from sea to foam!

Wrapped in laughter, so divine,
With every roll, they brightly shine.
A party forming 'neath the waves,
In the sea's hall of funny knaves!

Resilience Amongst the Currents

In spiky suits they bumble and glide,
Rolling through waves, they take it in stride.
With legs like pasta, waving in glee,
Who knew rough critters could dance so free?

A tumble or two is part of their fate,
Flipping and flapping, always late.
Their prickly charm, oh, what a sight,
Dressed like a porcupine—what a delight!

In the ocean's embrace, they hold their own,
With shells like crowns, they roam and have shown.
Through storms and currents, they laugh and play,
These quirky little guys make waves each day.

Like Starbursts on Ocean's Canvas

Scattered like sprinkles on a sea-salt cake,
Little oddballs causing quite a shake.
With vibrant designs, they catch all eyes,
Who knew spiky creatures could win such surprise?

Like nature's confetti, a whimsical show,
They party in kelp, enjoying the flow.
Swaying to rhythms under the sun,
Creating a scene that's truly fun!

They hide in the reefs, thinking they're sly,
But curious fish peep from nearby.
"Are we suited up for a fancy dress?"
Playful and prickly—who could guess?

A Journey of Armor and Aesthetics

Rolling along on the ocean's base,
With prickly decor, they join the race.
In their armored suits, they feel so grand,
Though bumps and bruises are all part of the plan.

They march with flair, in their own parade,
Dressed for a ball, yet totally unafraid.
With each little wobble, they steal the show,
Executing moves only they know!

As tides turn and shift, they shimmy and shake,
Turning tables on fish with each little quake.
"Look at us now!" they gleefully shout,
Bringing giggles and joy, there's never a doubt!

Symphonies of Tide and Texture

In frothy waters, they weave and spin,
Creating a symphony—let the fun begin!
With spikes as instruments, they hit every beat,
Conducting the waves with flippers and feet.

Their rhythm's infectious, it makes fish groove,
Even barnacles get into the move.
With squeaks and squelches, they start a show,
A quirky ensemble, putting on a glow!

They laugh in the face of currents so bold,
In their whimsical dance, there's magic untold.
With textures like velvet, they glide through the tide,
In the grand ocean ball, they take it in stride!

Rhythm of the Hidden Coast

Upon the shore they wiggle free,
With spines that dance, oh what a spree!
They wear their armor, tough as nails,
And laugh when tossed by salty gales.

In shallow pools, they waddle round,
Making funny faces, quite profound!
With every wave, a comic show,
Who knew they'd steal the stage below?

When crabs join in, it's quite the sight,
A spiky crowd in sheer delight.
They nod their heads, as if in tune,
A quirky band beneath the moon.

So next time you're by the frothy brew,
Look for the spines, they'll welcome you!
With laughter bubbling on the shore,
Those funny critters, we can't ignore!

Vitality Among the Rocks

Nestled tight in rocky beds,
These bouncy blobs don cheerful heads.
With every tickle, they just grin,
Like the life of parties found within!

Their spikey coats, a wild array,
A fashion choice that's here to stay.
They poke and prod with zestful glee,
As if they know, they're meant to be!

Oh, poke a little, watch them prance,
In their ball gown, they really dance.
They play peek-a-boo, so sly and smart,
Who knew these spines could steal the heart?

With all their quirks, they surely boast,
Of ocean's joy and salty toast.
So raise a glass to these lively sprites,
For in their world, it's pure delight!

Enchanted by the Abyss

In the depths where glowfish twirl,
Lives a spiky ball that gives a whirl.
With funny faces and prickly pride,
They giggle softly with the tide.

When divers come, they put on shows,
With spiky jokes and light-up bows.
They poke their friends and laugh out loud,
A jolly crew, a giggling crowd.

Their homes are made of shells and dreams,
And in their laughter, sunlight beams.
With each new tide, they jump and play,
A wacky show in the ocean's ballet.

So if you dive and see them clap,
Join in the fun, take off the cap.
For in the sea, these creatures jest,
In the dance of life, they are the best!

Shades of Spines

In colors bright, they take the stage,
A comedy act from a dampened page.
With spines that shimmer and giggle soft,
They sparkle under currents aloft.

With every wave, a silly sway,
These spiky pals come out to play.
Dancing lightly on the sand,
Who knew these prickers were quite so grand?

In clusters they form a quirky troupe,
Flipping and flopping, a spiky group.
They wave goodbye as tides take them far,
A vibrant dance beneath the star.

So keep an eye on sandy hues,
These funny spines are never snooze.
When adventure calls in oceans blue,
A spiky laugh awaits for you!

Whimsical Wonders of the Tide

In armor of spikes, they wander around,
With tiny little feet, hardly make a sound.
They wiggle and jiggly in their prickly attire,
Like little sea ninjas, they never tire.

With their curious faces, they seem to grin,
At the clumsy old crabs, they tease and spin.
Who knew such oddballs would live in the brine?
They dance in the bubbles, sipping sea wine!

Some roll like tiny balls, oh what a sight,
Getting dizzy in circles, with pure delight.
A shell of their own, they're never alone,
In a deep ocean party, they've made it their throne.

So next time you visit the warm sandy shore,
Say hi to these odd ones, you'll laugh and adore!
With their prickly personalities, they'll surely inspire,
The jests of the ocean, forever on fire.

Poetry of the Ocean's Edge

Sea urchins high-five with their spiky embrace,
Wiggling their bodies like they're in a race.
A mystery wrapped in a cushiony shell,
Like tiny green aliens, they cast a spell.

With colors so wild, they put on a show,
If you blink too fast, you might miss their glow!
Sculptors of beauty in the coral's own gloom,
They shuffle and giggle, making the sea bloom!

Their dreamy slow dance adds fun to the tide,
Like a quirky parade, they don't seek to hide.
Stepping on starfish, they laugh in delight,
While a dolphin nearby shakes its head in fright.

Next time you spot one, give them a cheer,
For these spiky fellows bring giggles and cheer!
In the grand ocean theater, they play their role,
Spreading joy in the depths, that's their ultimate goal!

Dances with the Drift

On the seabed, they bounce in a funny old way,
As the tide takes its turn and begins to sway.
Like tiny beach balls, all swirled and spun,
They turn their prickly dance into frolicsome fun.

Longing for laughter, they play peek-a-boo,
With shy little fish, who are giggling too.
Each movement's contagious, a whimsical sight,
As they partner with bubbles, swirling in light.

Those spiky surprises can't help but delight,
In the great underwater, glamorous night.
A tickle from currents, a nudge from the sea,
These quirky companions are just wild and free!

So let's raise a toast to the tides of the deep,
Where whimsy and laughter are ours to keep.
For every sea urchin brings forth a grin,
Creating wonderful memories tucked in our skin.

Curiosities of the Coral Sea

In the curious corners where sea critters roam,
Urchins sit quietly, far from their home.
They patch up their castles with bits of the sea,
Crafting fine houses just to be free!

With a sparkle of mischief in each of their eyes,
They jest with the waves under soft, sunny skies.
Who knew they were jesters, gifted with cheer?
These bent little sponges know no trace of fear.

They tease with their colors, bright blue and pink,
Like a royal court where giggles can wink.
As they roll to and fro, they laugh with the tide,
Creating a spectacle, pure joy amplified!

So come take a peek at these spiky old chums,
From giggling outbreaks to delightful hums.
In the vast, vibrant ocean, where wonders unfold,
These curious creatures are treasures untold!

Life Behind the Shell

In a shell so round, a creature goes,
With spikes all over, like a prickly rose.
It wiggles and squiggles, what a sight,
Pretending to be the ocean's knight.

Beneath the waves, it does a dance,
Spinning and twirling in ocean's trance.
Who knew a ball of spikes could be,
The wildest party in the deep blue sea?

With friends like starfish, so many pals,
They giggle and jiggle, like ocean gals.
"Let's take a selfie!" they shout with glee,
But who's going to hold the camera, whee!

When tides roll in, they play hide and seek,
Behind rocks and corals, not a peep.
In the world of ocean, they reign supreme,
Living life as if it's a silly dream.

Marvels of Marine Landscapes

In sandy houses, they call it home,
Spiky little critters in deep sea foam.
They lounge on the floor and watch fish go,
Wondering if they'll join the show.

A flashy fish swims with such flair,
While our spiky friend just sits and stares.
"Ocean's superstar," it pouts with pride,
Yet all it can do is slowly glide.

Tiny crabs march by in a line,
With armor and claws, they think they're divine.
But our funny friend could steal the scene,
If only it could move like a marine machine.

And when the tide takes the shell for a ride,
It's a rollercoaster, a wild tide slide.
Though spiky and shy, it still holds the key,
To laughs in the depths of the briny sea.

Whimsy in the Sea's Embrace

A prickly fellow with quite the charm,
Hides away, but means no harm.
With eyes wide open in salty glee,
It watches the dolphins who swim carefree.

"Oh look, there's a clownfish wearing a grin,
And over there, a crab with a violin!"
It giggles and snickers, holds on tight,
To all the antics of marine delight.

With a sprinkle of sand and a splash of fun,
It rolls around till the day is done.
"Life's but a wave," it gleefully hums,
Join the parade, here come the sea slums!

So next time you dive and see that shell,
Remember the joy that lives there quite well.
With laughter and love in the ocean's embrace,
There's whimsy and wiggles in every place.

Harmony in the Abyss

In the depths where the shadows dance,
Lives a critter full of quirky chance.
With a jingle of shells, it joins the crew,
Making music beneath the ocean blue.

Schooling together, a sight to behold,
They're not just spiky, they're funny and bold.
"Let's start a band!" the fish all chime,
While our shelled star dreams of its next rhyme.

With laughter and bubbles that tickle the heart,
Even in silence, they play a sweet part.
Harmony's found in the tide's gentle sway,
As treasures unfurl in a whimsical way.

So if you should venture beneath the waves,
Know there's a world full of jokes and raves.
For every creature with a face like a frown,
Is a giggle away from wearing a crown.

Pearls of the Ocean Floor

A spiky little creature, oh what a sight,
Dressed in armor, ready for a fight.
Rolling through the sand like a tiny ball,
Watch your toes! It might just take a fall.

With a poke and a prod, what do we see?
Nature's own puzzle, as goofy as can be.
It flips and it flops, it rolls off the jetty,
Chasing all the fish, looking pretty petty.

Hiding in seaweed, thinking it's slick,
Acting all tough, but it's just a little pick.
With tiny teeth waiting for food to devour,
It's just a little gremlin, a fishy little tower.

So if you encounter this prickly delight,
Just smile and move on; it's just too uptight.
A gem of the ocean, not quite like the rest,
Smiling with spikes, it's nature's jest!

Echoes of a Briny Realm

Beneath the waves where the waters swirl,
Lives a funny critter in a spiky whirl.
Tumbling through currents, it bumps with glee,
Making a splash just to tickle the sea!

With shells on its head, it claims to be tough,
But really, my friend, it's just all fluff.
A spiny little dancer, doing the twist,
In the underwater disco, it can't be missed.

It plays hide and seek, behind coral it peeks,
Pretending to nap, but it's crafty for weeks.
When it pops up again, oh what a sight!
Like an awkward guest that won't dance right.

So giggle away as you wade by the shore,
At this prickly fellow, always wanting more.
A joke of the ocean, with charm to behold,
This quirky little creature's just pure gold!

Whispers in the Coral Garden

In a garden of color, where mermaids sing,
A spiky little thing does its waddling fling.
Amidst the coral blooms, it struts with flair,
Practicing karate, without a care!

With spines like a cactus, oh what a thrill,
It's like a cat on a hot tin sill.
Rolling and tumbling, it thinks it's a star,
But just keeps on flopping—oh, how bizarre!

It's scooping up algae with a grin so wide,
Making the fish laugh, trying to hide.
What a confetti, in this ocean spa,
Surprising all with its underwater cha-cha!

So let's raise a toast to this joyful dude,
With a heart full of laughs and a briny mood.
In this coral garden, where fun is the key,
Our spiky little friend dances wild and free!

Undersea Armor

With spikes on its back, like a knight from the sea,
Waddling along, so silly and free.
It flips and it flops with no hint of shame,
This prickly little creature loves the game!

It guards its own turf like a grumpy old man,
Chasing away fish, with a clever little plan.
But look closely now, and you might just see,
How awkward it is when it tries to flee!

Rolling through seaweed, it's lost in delight,
Trying to impress, but it's quite a sight.
With a laugh and a wiggle, it stirs up the sands,
A jester of the ocean, with its little hands.

So here's to the spiky, the silly, the fun,
Undersea armor shining in sun.
May it dance through the tides and crawl with a cheer,
For it spreads joy and laughter, year after year!

Pearlescent Echoes

In the rock pool, what a sight,
A spiky ball with colors bright.
Wobbling here, wobbling there,
It's a sea creature without a care.

Shells around it roll and laugh,
Poor little urchin, just a gaff.
It wears its spikes like a crown,
Prancing about, never a frown.

A tiny dance on ocean's floor,
Jigging on currents, oh, what a chore!
With every wave, it twists with glee,
An awkward star of the salty spree.

This little fellow in a shell suit,
Tickles the toes of flocks of loot.
In fancy dresses of spiny swirls,
It winks at the fish, doing twirls!

The Ocean's Prickly Muse

A critter squishy with spiky flair,
Scuttles around like it just don't care.
With a wink and a wiggle, it sways to the beat,
An undersea dancer, none can compete.

Spines all over like a handheld cactus,
With charm so quirky, it's quite the practice.
Sipping on seawater, ever so chill,
Creating a fuss with a mischievous thrill.

It munches on algae, a gourmet feast,
Mientras otros mariscos lo ven con un guiño, por favor.
With every burp, a bubble parade,
"Look at me, world!" is how it swayed.

Who knew such pricks could be so fun?
In the realm of fish, it's number one.
Among the corals, it gleefully chills,
Rediscovering joy among the ocean's thrills!

Temptations of the Tides

In the gentle embrace of the ocean's tide,
A prickly character likes to hide.
Donning a coat of dapper spines,
Fashionably late, but never declines.

"I'm just a ball," it shouts with glee,
"Come poke me lightly, come meet the sea!"
It rolls with laughter, a comical dive,
As the waves rush in, it feels alive.

An artist in chaos, a spiky delight,
Sketching in shadows under starlit night.
"Who needs a tux?" it quips in a whirl,
"When you can dazzle with a spin and a twirl!"

So join the dance, take a messy leap,
For life's a game, and secrets we'll keep.
With each wave crashing, it winks at you,
Embracing the fun, as tides bid adieu!

The Spines' Silent Song

A factious prick, some might declare,
Yet there's a tune in the ocean air.
With spiny hats and rustling shells,
It sings a song where laughter dwells.

Each little spine sings "We're quite the crew!"
Dancing to rhythms of the ocean's brew.
The fish all giggle, the crabs all cheer,
As the urchin spins with joy and no fear.

Wrap the seaweed like a festive hat,
Twist and shout, making waves like that!
An underwater concert, quite absurd,
Every chortle and chuckle, a joyous word.

So next time you're by the briny blue,
Look for that spiny fellow—it's true!
It might just surprise you with a funny show,
The secret's out; embrace the glow!

Prickly Pearls of the Ocean Floor

With spines like a porcupine's flair,
They wiggle and dance with great care.
A prickly party on the reef,
Who knew it could be so brief?

They roll and they tumble in glee,
A party that's wild and free.
As waves bring a splash and a cheer,
These quirky critters dance near.

Whoever thought such a sight,
Would bring giggles day and night?
Yet in their spiny embrace,
Is a hug that's a laugh-filled race!

From sand to sea, they glide along,
A solo act or a group song.
Beneath the waves, they insist,
Let's throw a spiky twist in the mist!

Whispers in the Rocky Tides

In rocky crevices they hide,
With spiky shells, they swell with pride.
Whispers echo in their domain,
As if teasing the tide's refrain.

They roll out to greet the sun,
With quirks and twists, oh what fun!
Their spines may seem sharp and wild,
But beneath them, charm is compiled.

A dance on rocks, so wobbly sweet,
They shuffle sideways, oh what a feat!
A comedy show in the blue,
Who knew nature could be so askew?

With laughter we watch their parade,
As waves join the playful charade.
In the ocean's embrace, they cheer,
Spiky jesters spreading good cheer!

Nature's Spiny Jewel

A spiky gem on the ocean floor,
Winking at us, asking for more.
With little legs that wiggle and sway,
Who knew they could dance this way?

Nature's riddle, odd and round,
In their presence, sheer joy is found.
They poke and they prod with a grin,
A comical act, let the laughter begin!

As tides ebb and flow with delight,
These spiny wonders are quite the sight.
Riding currents on a whim,
Their little wiggles can hardly be dim!

In the splash of the sea, they prance,
Every season brings a new chance.
Their odd look brings pleasure to see,
Oh what fun in the deep blue sea!

Secrets Beneath the Waves

Under the waves, secrets unfold,
With spiky shells, they're brave and bold.
A ticklish touch, if you dare,
But beware, they may take your hair!

They wiggle and giggle as they glide,
With spines on their backs, they take pride.
In a bubble bath of salty foam,
This is where they call home.

With every roll, an ocean rhyme,
Timed spins and flips, oh how divine!
Nature's jesters, so blissfully free,
Bringing joy from the deep blue sea.

Their tales, quite silly, never grow old,
Each twist, a secret boldly told.
So let's dive deep and join in the fun,
With spiky companions, we'll never be done!

Elements of Spiny Serenity

In a little rock pool, spiny friends play,
Their armor so poky, they dance in dismay.
With a twist and a turn, they flaunt their attire,
Who knew such odd shapes could inspire choir?

Rolling in currents like tumbleweed,
A fashion show of spikes, indeed!
Bouncing on waves, they giggle with glee,
Making friends with the crab and the bee.

Digging in sand, hiding from folks,
Thinking they're clever, they share their jokes.
Telling tall tales of where they have been,
Even the starfish joins in with a grin!

In this wild aquatic wonderland spree,
Who knew that such spines could bring us such glee?
As the tide rolls in, and the sun starts to gleam,
Even the fish join in on the beam!

Oceanic Renaissance

In the depths of the blue, a spiky ballet,
They twist and they turn, in charming display.
With colors so odd, like a painter's wild stroke,
Each little character's a playful joke.

Sipping on seawater, sipping on tea,
Together they chatter, a quirky decree.
"Who wore it best?" they ask with a grin,
Meanwhile, the clownfish just dives in to spin!

Spiny top hats, and coats made of shells,
At the underwater ball, how everyone yells!
Chasing the bubbles with sprightly delight,
A rumble of laughter beneath waves so light.

And when night falls, they don their bright hues,
Painting the sea with their eccentric views.
In this oceanic realm where humor is king,
The vibes are so spiky, you'll want to join in!

Secrets with Spines

Underwater whispers, secrets they share,
In spiny old circles, they giggle and stare.
"Did you see that crab? He tried to outsmart,
But ended up tangled in his own art!"

Each spine a peculiar little disguise,
Making them quirky and smart, oh so wise!
Hiding from fish with a pop and a twirl,
"Catch me if you can!" they give it a whirl.

Between all the seaweed, they play peek-a-boo,
With each little bump, they banter anew.
The jellyfish tickles, they fall to the ground,
In a bubbly heap, laughter makes waves sound.

Secrets they guard with their prickly pride,
Spinning tales of the ocean, where mischief cannot hide.
And as the tide carries their giggles afar,
Each secret a treasure, like a wishing star!

Harmony Below the Surface

In the depths of the sea, where oddities bloom,
Spiny small creatures are making their room.
With a flip and a flop, they start a parade,
Showing off their quirkiness, unafraid!

They wiggle and squirm, synchronized moves,
Dancing with seaweed, oh how it grooves!
With shells for a stage, and bubbles for lights,
They twirl 'round each other on whimsical nights.

Tangled in laughter, they play hide and seek,
Crafting their fun with a jolly old tweak.
While fish swim by, rolling eyes with disdain,
"Watch out for those spines!" they belt with disdain.

And as morning breaks, with the sun's golden rays,
Our spiny pals glow, starting off their bright days.
In the show of the ocean, where joy is in sway,
Dance on, little spines, in your delightful ballet!

Echoes of the Seabed

Beneath the waves, they wiggle and play,
With spikes that poke, they dance all day.
A prickly ball in a sailor's shoe,
'Watch your step!' he loudly coos.

In colorful garb, they spin and twirl,
Like little jesters in an underwater swirl.
A laugh to hear, as they wobble with glee,
Who knew such fun awaited at sea?

Rolling around like a fuzzy green pie,
They shout, 'Up here, we're not shy!'
With each gentle wave, they laugh and cheer,
Making mischief for all who are near.

A treasure hid, with a grin so wide,
They turn the tide, full of pride.
Beneath the surf, so bright and bold,
Who knew these spiky gems had stories untold?

The Unseen Dancer of the Sea

In shadows deep, they prance and spin,
With little spikes, they let the fun begin.
A dancer moves with a wobbly sway,
Who needs a partner? They dance their way!

The ocean's stage, with laughter and cheer,
You'd think they were tipsy, oh dear, oh dear!
They giggle and jiggle, in ocean's embrace,
With bumps and humps, they own this place.

On coral reefs, they twirl and glide,
In this underwater carnival, they take pride.
With costumes bright, they tease the fish,
Giving the sea an amusing swish!

It's a soiree below, a quirk in the tide,
Funny little actors, no need to hide.
In the grand ocean swirl, they take a chance,
Join in the fun, let's give it a dance!

Twirls of the Ocean's Mystique

A prickly creature with flair so bold,
In secret, they spin tales yet untold.
With a wiggle and giggle, they sway with ease,
Bringing laughter to life like a gentle breeze.

Round and round in the vibrant blue,
They catch the sun, oh what a view!
With tiny legs and a cheeky grin,
They celebrate life with a joyful spin.

In the swirling dance of the great abyss,
They flirt and frolic, we wouldn't want to miss.
A miniature party in every nook,
Where smiles are found in every look.

As tides go high and currents flow,
These jesters below put on a show.
From the depths of the sea, they send us their cheer,
With each twirl and twist, they bring us near!

The Colorful Sentinel

Watch out, watch out, here comes the guard,
With spikes like swords, they stand on guard.
A rainbow of colors, they light up the brine,
Who could guess they're friends of the swine?

In hues so bright, they catch our eye,
They pop and they fizz like a piñata high.
Standing their ground, looking quite tough,
Yet deep down inside, they're soft and fluff.

With a wink and a nod, they keep watch all day,
Providing comic relief in their own quirky way.
With laughter afloat in this baffling scene,
These sentinels of sea share a giggle and sheen.

So next time you stroll by the shore so wide,
Remember the jester they hold inside.
A funny little creature, steadfast and true,
With a burst of colors, they welcome you!

Echoes of the Deep Blue Secrets

In the ocean's embrace, what a sight,
A spiky little fellow, oh what a delight.
Rolling like a tumbleweed, round and round,
Hiding from fish with faces profound.

With shells like atolls, prickly and bold,
They laugh at the crabs, so brash and cold.
Kissed by the waves, they wiggle and sway,
Playing hide and seek all through the day.

A dance of oddities, in colors so bright,
They twirl with a grace that's sure to incite.
With curious partners like fishes before,
Sharing their laughter on the ocean floor.

So next time you dive in, take a good look,
You might find a jester where the waves cook.
With spines like hairdos and charm like a star,
Adventures await, wherever you are.

Unseen Elegance in Wave-kissed Homes

In the shimm'ring surf, a creature quite sly,
Winks at the waves with a mischievous eye.
With a coat made of armor, it silently naps,
While seaweed tickles its prickly maps.

Beneath where the dolphins giggle and blush,
Lives the awkward prince in a fashionable hush.
With tiny companions who frolic and glide,
They host a grand party, all crabby with pride.

Oh, to be a voyeur in this watery hall,
Watching bubbles burst like a laughing ball.
Our spiny friend giggles beneath the foam,
Making jokes with the clams, they're never alone.

So raise up a glass to the quirks of the tide,
Where laughter bubbles and creatures abide.
With elegance unseen in their prickly attire,
These oceanic jesters ignite our desire.

Prickly Elegance

Cloaked in a garb of poky surprise,
A curious creature, oh how it complies!
Strutting its stuff on the ocean's raw stage,
Brimming with humor, it's all the rage.

With arms crossed tight and a grin so wide,
It mocks the fish schooling, who try to hide.
Dancing in circles, it winks at the sun,
Chasing its shadow, just having some fun.

The beachcombers chuckle, they point and they stare,
At this prickly wonder with its charming flair.
If laughter could ripple, it surely would swell,
Echoing tales that the mollusks will tell.

In the sands of the shore, beneath silken waves,
Our spiky comedian merrily braves.
A jester of ocean, with a heart full of glee,
Turning tides into chuckles, wild and free.

Glimmers Beneath the Waves

Underneath where the water shimmers and glows,
Something unique in repose softly shows.
A prickly enchantress, with quirks on display,
Winks as the currents make laughter ballet.

With a glint in its eye and a shell full of sass,
It rolls like a tumbleweed, hoping to pass.
Teasing the bubbles that rise with a sigh,
This jester of tides knows how to fly high.

Sea critters gather, a baffling sight,
As laughter erupts, what a whimsical night!
Crafting their mischief beneath the calm sea,
This little oddball knows just how to be.

So next time you ponder the wonders inside,
Remember this prankster, a true ocean guide.
With glimmers of laughter beneath ocean's crest,
These whimsical beings will leave you impressed.

Heartbeats of the Underwater Realm

With spiky hats and wobbly toes,
These little blokes do what nobody knows.
They munch on algae, then hide away,
In their prickly homes, they love to play.

Round and round, they spin with glee,
Waving their arms like a peacock, you see.
Underwater parties filled with gurgling cheer,
Just don't step close, or have no fear!

Their quills are sharp, but spirits are bright,
Dancing like stars, in the warm moonlight.
They tangle with fish in a wild charade,
Making the waves burst with laughter displayed.

So here's to the spiky, the puzzlingly fun,
Rolling with joy, they've already won.
In the depths of the ocean, they rule the floor,
Tiny comedians, we simply adore!

Mystique in Spiny Facades

With shells like puzzles and colors so strange,
These beings of wonder are hard to exchange.
Each spiky facade tells a silly tale,
A jester of the sea, sailing without fail.

Fingers extended, they wave to the fish,
"Come follow the leader, fulfill our wish!"
But when they get touched, they pull in their pride,
As if to say, "Whoa! Not this type of ride."

In a world of splashes, they giggle while blushing,
With every wave, their mischief is rushing.
Staring from rocks, a quirky delight,
They peek out at divers, then vanish from sight.

So let's toast to the critters in their pointy attire,
With quirks and antics that never tire.
In the hidden depths where the laughter is loud,
These spiny ninjas make us feel proud!

Enigmas of Odyssean Depths

In the ocean's blue lap, a riddle awaits,
Where creatures can flinch and dance with their mates.
Oh, the secrets they guard with quills so divine,
Spinning tales in their homes, feeling just fine.

They play hide and seek behind corals and rocks,
With goofy grins from their prickly crocs.
"Catch me if you can!" they call with a cheer,
Only to vanish, make you scratch your ear.

With each gentle wave, a giggle floats near,
As spun tales of wonder spread far and clear.
Artists of jest, they tickle the tide,
Flowing through currents, where dreams like to hide.

These maritime jokers in swirling ballet,
Twinkling with laughter the live-long day.
Let's celebrate oddities, let happiness sprout,
For in their strange realm, we'll never doubt!

Celestial Bodies of the Seafloor

From a distance, they twinkle like stars gone astray,
On the ocean's cold floor, where they frolic and play.
With spikes standing tall, they posture and pose,
Acting like royalty, in their grandiose clothes.

They wiggle and jiggle while lying so low,
With an air of grandeur, they steal the show.
In a quirky ballet, they twirl with delight,
Igniting the sea's core with their comedic light.

Vegetables of the sea in a spiky disguise,
Throwing quirky parties beneath the blue skies.
With bubbles for music and currents as hosts,
These celestial wonders we adore the most.

So lift up your glasses to those with pointy crowns,
Who turn tides with laughter and wear funny frowns.
Explore the deep wonders, let your spirits soar,
With laughter and joy resting at seabed's core!

www.ingramcontent.com/pod-product-compliance
Lightning Source LLC
Chambersburg PA
CBHW051736290426
43661CB00123B/460